SING! D TO SING, EVEN AT "NIGHT"

Receiving Supernatural Results by Singing Even in Adversity

Buisi Udom

ISBN: 987-1-9160574-2-5

First published in Great Britain by TUEMS Publishing in 2019
TUEMS Publishing is a division of TUEMS Limited
www.tuemspublishing.co.uk

A CIP record for this book is available from the British Library

Dedication

I dedicate this book to:
God Almighty, The only wise and true God.
My lovely family and friends.
Those who are going through a night situation.
All those who stood by me during the recent
night situation experience I had.

Contents

Acknowledgements

I acknowledge My Lord and Saviour, Jesus Christ. My wonderful counsellor, The Holy Spirit who is my greatest Teacher, who teaches me all things. My Father and my God, Almighty God. Omniscience, omnipotent, the only wise God. To you be all the glory.

I give honour to whom honour is due by acknowledging, my father in the Lord, Brother Emma Okorie, the President of Living Word Ministries International, where I was trained and equipped in line with the vision of the Ministry "Equipping Believers for the work of their Ministries". I also learnt that the supernatural can be taught. The spiritual training and impartation I received under you, sir and this great Ministry right from my youth, equipped me greatly to face my future.

Right from when I was a teenager, I adored, my mother in the Lord, Sister Chi Emma Okorie, Administrator, LWM; President, Unique Women; Rector, Living Word training Centre, who was also my instructor at the Living Word Training Centre on the course "Music and the Believer". Sister Chi, you imparted so much in me as a worshipper, which eventually led to my realisation of my calling especially in the Music ministry. One of the most important things I learnt from you is that praising and worshipping God is not an act or occasional experience, but a life-style.

To my pastors that groomed me from the time I got born-again, as a young believer in Christ; Pastor (Dr.) Jude Ehiemere and His lovely wife, Mrs. Esther Ehiemere, who is my role model right from when I was a young believer growing up in Christ. I love you. You and your family inspired me greatly.

Pastor Israel Nwobilor, Pastor Abraham and Pastor (Mrs.) Iheoma Nwobilo, the counsels I received from you, growing -up in the Lord has helped me immensely in life. Thank you.

Thank you, Rev. (Dr.) Paul Abolo, my older brother, for your encouragement to me and for buying for me, my first Saxophone, while I was pursuing my University degree in Music.

Rev. Dan Mba Uka, I appreciate you so much for praying for me and with me, especially in adversity.

Special thanks to my Biological parents, Mr. Paul A. Abolo and especially my Mother, Mrs. Theodora Abolo. Mother, nothing can erase the mental picture I have of you right from my childhood, kneeling in prayer, singing praises and worshipping God always, which to me underscores the importance of prayers and singing praises to God. You made so much impact in me and you are a great source of inspiration and encouragement to me even in adversity. I love you.

I esteem highly and appreciate the Leadership and membership of the Bridge Church, Bolton, United Kingdom. Our life group leaders, Pat and Sam Tuplin, thank you for your Agape love and care.

My profound regards to my childhood friend and sister in the Lord, Pastor (Mrs.) Linda Nweke and her Husband, Pastor Uche Nweke, you both inspired me greatly and helped to make this vision of my "Book Publishing Project" materialize. Thank you and Special thanks to Pastor Sunday Akinteye and his lovely wife, Elizabeth Akinteye, My Publishers.

Words are not enough to express how I love and cherish my musical family, which I believe is answer to my heartfelt prayers to God and a divine gift from God to me, in line with the fulfilment of our divine destiny especially in the music ministry. I appreciate you greatly, My Husband, Nnamso - my love, and My beautiful daughters, Sarah, Esther, Shalom, Precious and Blossom. Thank you all for being there for me always.

Foreword

My wife Linda and I have known Evangelist Buisi and her husband for over twenty years. They are true servants of the Lord. They are worshippers to the core. And they have travelled far and wide ministering, mentoring and equipping believers. In particular, I will always remember the difference they made at my 50th birthday celebration. So, what you will read in this book is what we have seen Evangelist Buisi and her family live-out over time.

Sing! Dare to Sing, Even at "Night" is a much-needed book based on the near-death experience of the author. In my view, its unique appeal is that it touches a chord which I think will resonate with Christians around the world. I am a witness to the fact that the message of hope and joyful expectation that the book brings can be life changing. Four months after Linda and I got married, I became very sick. It was indeed a night season for us that continued for over a year. I believe a major turning point in my recovery occurred one particular night as I lay in bed. I was in so much pain, and my body was urging me to scream out in pain. But within me, a bubble of laughter was forming. And, what was my response? I dared to laugh! I wish I had been laughing and singing right from the start of the ill-health. I imagine I would have had a quicker recovery.

The Psalm contain many songs written during night seasons. Jesus sang with His disciples before He was betrayed and crucified. Paul and Silas dared to sing at midnight while in prison. And the amazing testimony that is the background to this book is that Evangelist Buisi and her family also dared to sing on the eventful day she almost died. However, as the author clearly points out, 'Dare to Sing' is not just an act; it is not meant to be a one-time event. Rather it is the continual expression of a heart that trusts the Lord especially in challenging times. So, in times of crisis; when trouble comes; when you are afflicted–if you are experiencing what could be called a night season–and even if you are happy, I encourage you to dare to sing.

As I think of people in recent history who have modelled this life-style, I remember Fanny Crosby. Fanny was blind. Yet she wrote hundreds of hymns including *Blessed Assurance, Jesus Is Mine*. And what was the reason for her songs in the night? One word. One name. Jesus! She was longing for that New Day when her eyes will be opened to see the Master face to face. In like manner, I urge you to lift your eyes from the issues around you and keep them fixed on the Lord. Think about His promises and let faith rise up in your heart. Sing a new song to Him as you behold His beauty. And keep your mouth filled with songs of praise as you call-out your morning. This is the pathway to the dawning of the new day you desire.

Uche Nweke

Author, Senior Pastor Quality Life Church London

Introduction

Have you ever been in that situation where life circumstances are so tough, where everything around you is saying, weep? And in spite of all, the Spirit of God says, "Sing praises to God" and you chose to sing instead of weeping? Then you are not alone. *Sing! Dare to Sing, even at 'Night'* is a reality to me today. It is not just another book title. As you read on, you will find the story of how this sacrifice of the lips to God made a remarkable difference in our home at a time of crisis.

The Scripture tells us in James 5:13, "...is anyone happy? Let them sing songs of praise." It is very natural, as easy as eating a piece of cake or a walk in the park to sing songs of praise to God when you are happy; when everything is going well. However, to continue singing praises to God *when life happens*, at a time that can be called "Night", when you are going through adversities, it is a sacrificial service to God. That is sacrifice of praise indeed. Hebrews 13:15 says, *"Therefore by Him let us continually offer the sacrifice of praise to God, that is, the fruit of our lips, giving thanks to His name".*

Singing songs of praise to God is a proactive way of celebrating our God given victory in advance. Singing praises and worshiping God precedes miracles and every super-natural result. So do not put your ladder against the wrong wall by weeping all through a night situation experience. Instead, take a step of faith and sing! Dare to sing even at night. Choose to praise your way through the storms of life and whatever you *go through* and you will definitely achieve supernatural and uncommon results and Joy will surely come in the morning.

In the chapters ahead, you will learn about how to build your faith to sing in times of adversity, affliction and difficulty. You will also find the benefits of singing at night and the fact that great songs can come out of night situations. Yet, in saying the things above, it is important to keep in mind that we sing praises to God and worship Him because He is God; Not necessarily because of what He did for us or what we want Him to give to us. Revelations 4: 11 says that God created all things for His pleasure. I believe "all things" includes us all. So, give God pleasure by singing songs of praise to Him and by worshipping Him. Do it continually until it becomes your life-style. Remember, God loves consistency.

Buisi Udom

Chapter One

sound of singing praises to God

"Enter into His gates with thanksgiving, and into His courts with praise. Be thankful to Him, and bless His name." (Psalm 100:4)

The sound of the piano and the voice of singing by my family members woke me up that morning. It was time for our morning devotion. Although I am normally one of the first in the family to get to the living room for our time of giving thanks and praise to God, on this particular day I was so fatigued I overslept. The previous day was quite a hectic one for me. I slept late and did not even sleep well during the night for some reasons. I knew I had taken on so much to do at that particular time coupled with the "night" situation I was going through. I got so busy and was not eating well and resting well in that period. However, my yearning for God's presence and the desire to fulfil my vow to sing praises to Him all my life, propelled me to rise up and get going on my way to join my family in the living room.

My Background

Before continuing with the story of what happened that morning, I would like to share a little bit about my background. I became aware of the call of God on my life thirty years ago after I gave my life to Jesus and became a born-again Christian. Right from my youth, spending time with God in singing songs of praise and praying as well as meditating on the Word of God and soul winning became my passion. Since then I have been serving God especially in the Music Ministry within the body of Christ. I was ordained twenty – five years ago, as a Minister of God in the word of God and Music.

My family and I believe that God has called us to be a praise on earth for Him. To sing down the glory of God on earth. To sing and worship

God always in spirit and in truth. Hence, like me, my husband is an ordained minister of God, and a Music Minister too. Together we have raised our children to be ministers of God, especially through Music. By the grace of God, there is always the atmosphere of singing and worship in our home. And we are passionate about praising God no matter the situation we find ourselves in. We believe that singing songs of praise to God creates a greater awareness of Him and a stronger manifestation of His presence. This is because God dwells in the praises of His people.

As a family, we bought different kinds of musical instruments, like Keyboards, electric organs, guitar and so on that we use to praise God in our home. We also run a music ministry, where we teach and train other people. And we sing and minister in music in churches, Gospel concerts, and crusades globally. We have produced music Albums, which is available online to minister to people everywhere.

Returning to the Story

I got up though very tired and tried to rush out of bed. I was desperate to join my family members already singing songs of praise to God that eventful morning. In the process I felt a dizzy spell, missed my steps and landed on the floor. The bang from the fall was so loud that it called the attention of everyone in my house and all my family members ran upstairs to my room. While I was on the floor, I felt a very strong force moving my soul out of my body through something that I can describe as a tunnel. A very strong force on a very high speed. My body was on the floor, but I could feel my soul moving out of my body by this strange force that I cannot really explain more than I have already done. My husband and children ran upstairs towards me and about the same time I struggled to call the name of "Jesus" with all the faith and strength left in me. As I did this, my soul began coming back into my body. Indeed, it was a fight; a good fight of faith. And, Hallelujah! By faith, my spirit responded and my soul returned to my body.

My husband lifted my head up, while I was still sitting on the floor. And he and the children continued praying for me, calling and singing the name of Jesus. There was evidence of corporate anointing as they all joined faith together. It was an atmosphere of praise and worship to God. And I believe that because of this, God intervened and revitalized my mortal body. I believe the Spirit of Him that raised Jesus Christ from the dead, who lives in me, revitalized my mortal body, because my story is not over and I have not finished my God-given assignment.

Then I tried to open my eyes and asked for water still sitting on the floor, while my husband and children continued to sing and pray. I was taken to one of the best hospitals in England where I was given medical attention for hours to ascertain the cause of the fall and all that happened to me. My medical result said everything was fine. The doctors and medical personnel carried out every necessary test and medical examination, but found nothing wrong with me. When I became more curious, the doctors and medical personnel simply said it was a warning sign for stress. And advised that I reduce anything stressing me. But I believe God intervened, delivered me from death and healed me miraculously. What if I had passed on from the encounter? I asked myself.

My Heart Is Full of Thanks

Thank God for the faith to dare to sing even in a night situation. Thank God for the yearning and craving to fulfil my vow to sing praises to Him always and consistently all the days of my life. Thank God for my family's life-style of having morning devotion and singing praises to God always. I believe this created the atmosphere of worship and the manifestation of the presence of God.

Thank God for the name of Jesus, the name that is above every other name. "Wherefore, God also hath highly exalted Him, and given Him a name which is above every name, that at the name of Jesus every Knee should bow, of things in heaven, and things in earth and things under the earth..." Philippians 2:9-10

Thank God for His intervention. He is the sovereign God. Maybe I would have passed on during the encounter. But God intervened. God miraculously delivered me from death, healed me and refreshed me.

Although we believers in Christ Jesus recognise that to be absent from the body is to be with the Lord, I believe I still have a ministry to fulfil, more exploits to do for the Lord in soul winning, to care for my family and children, as well as other children and young people in the body of Christ that I teach and mentor. I still desire to see my children's children. Write more books and songs. Touch more lives. Make addition to knowledge through my academic doctoral research. Help humanity. Teach and lead others to sing for God and sing even some more.

I still want to proclaim and declare the word of God, make His praises known in all the earth and above all continue to sing for God. I strongly believe that it shall be done unto me according to my faith, Matthew 9:29.

"Now to Him who is able to do exceedingly abundantly above all that we ask or think, ***according to the power that works in us****, to Him be glory...". Ephesians 3:20-21.*

Chapter Two

singing at 'Night'

Tehillah is a Hebrew word which means *to sing*. "Sing" is a divine command, because there are over 300 Bible mandates to sing. Some examples are:

Psalm 96:1. "Sing to the Lord a new song; sing to the Lord, all the earth".

Psalm 95:1. "Come, let us sing for joy to the Lord,"

Psalm 33:3 "Sing to him a new song; play skilfully with a loud noise."

Psalm 98:1 O "sing to the LORD a new song; for he has done marvellous things: ..."

Psalm 149:1 "Praise you the LORD. Sing to the LORD a new song, and his praise ..."

1 Chronicles 16:23-33 "Sing to the LORD, all the earth; show forth from day to day his salvation..."

Revelation 5:9 "And they sung a new song, saying, You are worthy to take the book, ..."

Revelation 14:3 "And they sung as it were a new song before the throne, and before ..."

Psalm 67:3-6 "Let the people praise you, O God; let all the people praise you..."

Psalm 68:32 "Sing to God, you kingdoms of the earth; O sing praises to the Lord; Selah:"

God is our song

Psalm 89:1 says that God is our song, God is the words of our music. We sing praises to God and worship God because He is God. *Psalm 100:3 "Know ye that the LORD he is God: it is he that hath made us, and not we ourselves; we are his people, and the sheep of his pasture."* We sing praises to God and worship God, not because of what He did or what He did not do for us or give or will give us, but because He is God. Revelations 4:11 says that God created all things for His pleasure, I belief all things include us all. So let us give God pleasure by singing praises to Him and worshipping Him

Singing praises to God and worshiping God is done continuously in Heaven. (See Revelation 7:9-10). It is the norm and the Bible commands us to do same.

Divine Blessing, Exchange and Change:

SING; IS A DIVINE COMMAND, WHICH WHEN YOU OBEY, ATTRACTS DIVINE BLESSINGS.

Sing; is a divine command, which when you obey, attracts divine blessings. Psalm 59:16 says, *"I will sing of your strength; I will sing aloud of your steadfast love in the morning. For you have been to me a fortress and a refuge in the day of my distress."* Psalm 134:1-2 tells us, *"Come, bless the Lord all you servants of the Lord, who stand by* ***night*** *in the house of the Lord, lift up your hands, to the Holy place, and bless the Lord!"*

Night signifies affliction, adversity, persecution, tribulation, hardship, difficulty, danger, and different stormy situations people face in life. Some night situation experiences occur in the form of delays. Delay in receiving the promise of God for your life in a certain area. Delay in getting pregnant and giving birth to a child. Delay in getting your settlement in a foreign country. As well as delay in finding a job or changing to a new career. For some people, night situations may come in the form of prolonged ill health.

I could go on to give more examples of night situations. But when we take up the biblical command and dare to sing to God in our night situation, something remarkable and life-transforming happens. We are able by the grace of God to take charge of the situation we face and make a divine exchange that will change the situation. For those who dare to sing at night, it pleases God to give to them:

- A beautiful headdress, instead of ashes.
- Oil of gladness, instead of mourning.
- Garment of Praise, instead of a faint spirit.

Isaiah 61:3 says, *"To grant to those who mourn in Zion— to give them a beautiful headdress instead of ashes, the oil of gladness instead of mourning, the garment of praise instead of a faint spirit; that they may be called oaks of righteousness, the planting of the Lord, that he may be glorified."*

From Acts 16:23-35 we see that Paul and Silas experienced a divine exchange because they sang in their night situation. They were falsely accused, beaten, judged, condemned and put in prison, while they were doing the work of God. And in that critical situation, they prayed and sang songs of praise to God. They dared to sing songs of praise to God at midnight. They took charge of their situation by singing to God even though they were broken. And we know that a broken and contrite heart, God will not overlook (Psalm 51:16-17). Little wonder God could not over-look Paul and Silas. God intervened instantly, miraculously changed their situation, and the position of Paul and Silas changed. The jailor started calling them "Sirs". And the opportunity to witness, preach Christ and win souls for Christ emerged. Indeed, God can turn your captivity into captive when you dare to sing even at night.

GOD CAN TURN YOUR CAPTIVITY INTO CAPTIVE WHEN YOU DARE TO SING EVEN AT NIGHT.

Singing at Night is a Sacrifice of Praise indeed

SINGING PRAISES TO GOD DURING A "NIGHT" SITUATION IN YOUR LIFE IS A SACRIFICE. IT WILL COST YOU SOMETHING.

Notice from the experience of Paul and Silas that singing praises to God during a "night" situation in your life is a sacrifice. It will cost you something. It is a sacrifice of praise indeed. David said, I will not offer to God sacrifice that will cost me nothing. 2 Samuel 24:24.

Singing at Night Requires Faith and Perseverance

Paul and Silas exercised faith as well as perseverance in their night situation. They did not allow what they were "going through" to stop them from singing to God. Instead, they exercised their faith in God and were willing to endure hardship like good soldiers of Christ.

2 Timothy 2: "You therefore must endure hardship as a good soldier of Jesus Christ". To stand strong in faith and persevere in trying situations is a daring act. "Dare" means, to be bold, take up the challenge, to have the courage

to. Make a deliberate decision and resolution to dare to sing praises to God and worship God even at **night**. Believers in Christ Jesus who stay strong in faith and persevere in the face of trying night situations will be rewarded. We are encouraged to endure hardship as good soldiers of Christ. In his second letter to the Corinthian church, the apostle Paul points out that the night situations we go through are light afflictions compared to the weight of glory that they are working out for us – a glory that is yet to be revealed. *2 Corinthians 4:17 "For our light affliction, which is but for a moment, worketh for us a far more exceeding and eternal weight of glory"*

MAKE A DELIBERATE DECISION AND RESOLUTION TO DARE TO SING PRAISES TO GOD AND WORSHIP GOD EVEN AT NIGHT.

Habbakkuk 3:17-18 "though the fig tree does not bud and there are no grapes on the vines, though, the olive crops fails and the fields produce no food, though there are no sheep in the pen and no cattle in the stalls, Yet, I will rejoice in the Lord, I will be joyful in God my saviour." The "I will", demonstrates, a conscious effort and willingness, Intentional. The verse above also showcases faith and perseverance.

Chapter Three

Right perspective in a 'Night' situation

Night symbolises abandonment. A time of difficulty and adversity. And a time of weeping. From Psalm 30:5 we see that, "weeping may endure for a night...". However, having the right perspective will make you remember that joy comes in the morning: "Weeping may endure for a night, but joy comes in the morning" Psalm 30:5. You also need to have an *overcomer mind-set*. Jesus said in John 16:33, *"These things I have spoken to you, that in Me you may have peace. In the world you will have tribulation; but be of good cheer, I have overcome the world". John 16:33.*

Having the "overcomer mind-set" and the right perspective will make you sing praises to God instead of "putting your ladder against the wrong wall" by weeping throughout a "night" situation experience in your life. As you sing and worship, you will realize that it is a time to come boldly to the throne of grace and obtain mercy and everything you need to overcome. It is a time to be in a position where you can hear from God and receive solutions, vision and direction from Him. This will enable you to reposition yourself spiritually. Remember, the spiritual controls the physical. God has given us victory and we need to see our God-given victory and possess it.

Repositioning Yourself Spiritually

> YOUR POSITION DETERMINES YOUR PERCEPTION AND YOUR PERCEPTION IS IMPORTANT, BECAUSE YOU CAN ONLY GO AS FAR AS YOU CAN SEE.

Why reposition? Your position determines your perception and your perception is important, because you can only go as far as you can see. In Genesis 13:15 God told Abraham, "...as far as you can see". We read in 1 Corinthians 2:9-10 that, *"Eyes has not seen, nor ears heard, nor have entered into the heart of man, the things which God has prepared for those who love Him. But God has revealed them to us through His Spirit..."* God reveals things to us believers by His Spirit. The spiritual controls the physical. Spiritually repositioning yourself in the presence of God is very important, especially through singing praises to Him and worshipping Him. This will help you to begin to see yourself, spiritually, the way God sees you. God sees and speaks into our future destiny not our present circumstance. God sees and speaks into our future; where we are going and what we will become. I encourage you to look at God's promises. Do not trust what you see with your physical eyes. If you can see the God given vision of your life spiritually, then you will surely see the physical manifestation, hence the spiritual controls the physical.

Changed Perception: A Biblical Analogy

In Matthew 14:23-30 Jesus was walking on the water and Peter said to Him, Lord if it is you, tell me to come to you on the water. Jesus said "Come". Then Peter began to walk on the water towards Jesus. He did this looking unto Jesus and keeping his focus on Him. But when Peter saw the wind (the night situation), he was afraid and began to sink. Peter did not sink until he removed his focus from Jesus and began to see the wind and the waves. As long as Peter focused on Jesus, he walked on the water. Choose what you want to see. Focus on Jesus, not the "night" situation that you go through. Choose what you want to see. When Peter changed his perception by looking at the wind and the waves, instead of looking unto Jesus, he began to sink. Choose to look unto Jesus, the author and the finisher of our faith, your faith will increase and doubt will disappear. *"For we walk by faith, not by sight." 2 Corinthians 5:7.*

Personal Testimony

"The eyes of your understanding being enlightened; that ye may know what is the hope of his calling, and what the riches of the glory of his inheritance in the saints," Ephesians 1:18.

God showed me a mental picture of abundance, when I did not even have enough and could not physically see abundance. Now I do not just have enough, I have more than enough, and I am getting into the abundance that God showed me years back. Singing praises and worshipping God even in that night situation, changed my perception and helped me to refocus on God during the night situation. It enabled me to receive insights, far sight and foresight from God.

God said in the book of Isaiah 46:10 "From the beginning I predicted the outcome; long ago I foretold what would happen. I said that my plans would never fail, that I would do everything I intended to do."

You need to reposition yourself spiritually. Come boldly to the throne of Grace. Focus and look unto Jesus, the author and the finisher of our faith. Focus on God's promises. When you reposition yourself, you will achieve changed perception. God will give you a true vision of yourself – and that God-given vision of you and of your situation is the right perception of you. Your present situation will no longer define and control you, your mind-set and how you act. Rather the God given vision of you, will become your drive, motivate you to act by faith, keep you going and singing praises to God and worshipping Him, even in that night

GOD WILL GIVE YOU A TRUE VISION OF YOURSELF – AND THAT GOD–GIVEN VISION OF YOU AND OF YOUR SITUATION IS THE RIGHT PERCEPTION OF YOU.

situation until the physical manifestation of your God given vision of your life and victory!

God's Perspective of Us

Judges 6:12 "And the Angel of the Lord appeared to Gideon and said, "The Lord is with you, mighty warrior".

God was seeing Gideon as a mighty warrior when he was still hiding to thresh wheat by the winepress and hiding from the Midianites. When Gideon got the right perception of himself, his attitude changed. He began to see himself the way God sees him and he became the mighty warrior and the champion that God ordained him to be, instead of a fearful man. That is the right perspective.

God Is Omniscient and has Perception and Knowledge of the End from the Beginning

God sees and knows the end from the beginning. In the book of 1 Samuel 1:9-28 Hannah was praying for a son, when God was seeing her as the mother of several sons. Little wonder the bible commands the barren to sing: *"Sing, barren woman, you who never bore a child; burst into song, shout for joy, you who were never in labour; because more are the children..."* (Isaiah 54:1)

While we see the physical and the temporal things and circumstances around us, God who does not see as men see, looks at us in the future. God sees the future. That is why He wants us to be proactive and celebrate in advance. Take the challenge and sing praises to God, even in a night situation and you will be celebrating your God given victory in advance. *"For we walk by faith, not by sight." 2 Corinthians 5:7.*

In the previous chapter, we looked at the story of Paul and Silas who were put in prison for doing the work of the ministry. This was a "Night" situation experience for Paul and Silas, but daring to sing praises to God and to worship God in that night season situation, helped them to achieve changed perception. They repositioned themselves and began to see themselves the way God sees them. I belief they forgot, temporarily that they were in prison, as they sang so loud that other prisoners heard them. Singing praises to God and worshipping God during a night situation experience will help you achieve a change in perception;

getting the vision of yourself from God and you see yourself the way God sees you. And getting that vision of you and your future from God will make you sing praises to God even more and vice versa.

Perceive a Night situation as an Opportunity to manifest as a son of God

A NIGHT SITUATION EXPERIENCE CAN EITHER DRAW YOU CLOSER TO GOD OR FURTHER AWAY FROM HIM

A night situation experience can either draw you closer to God or further away from Him depending on how you see it (your perception). When you see it as an opportunity for God to come through for you and show His power on your behalf, you will love God more and you will sing praises to Him, instead of weeping. Also, when you perceive it as an opportunity for you to manifest as a son or daughter of God, the situation will draw you closer to God and you will sing praises to God. *"For the creation waits with eager longing for the revealing of the sons of God" Romans 8:19.*

Chapter Four

Experiencing the Manifestation of God's Presence

"...but be filled with the Spirit, addressing one another in psalms and hymns and spiritual songs, singing and making melody to the Lord with your heart, giving thanks always and for everything to God the Father in the name of our Lord Jesus Christ". (Ephesians 5:18-20)

Every believer baptised and filled with the Holy Spirit carries the presence of God in them. But some are not aware or are less aware of the presence of God. Creating the awareness and experiencing the manifestation of the presence of God is always important and awesome.

Singing praises to God and worshiping Him helps us to regain consciousness of His presence. And this makes it easier for us to experience the manifestation of the presence and power of God. (See 2 Kings 3:15-17).

SINGING PRAISES TO GOD AND WORSHIPING HIM HELPS US TO REGAIN CONSCIOUSNESS OF HIS PRESENCE.

Psalm 16:11 says, "...In His Presence is fullness of joy; at thy right hand are pleasures forevermore". In God's presence there is power, joy, peace, pleasure of experiencing and enjoying God. Experiencing the manifestation of God's presence leads to experiencing the greatness of God. The more you stay in God's presence by singing praises to Him and worshiping Him, the more you experience the manifestation of His presence and the consciousness of His mightiness. Every other thing like unfavourable circumstances that seemed like mountains before you begin to melt like wax.

Psalm 97:5 "The Mountains melt like wax at the presence of the LORD, At the presence of the Lord of the whole earth." And if you can perceive it and believe it, you will receive the manifestation of your miracle. Enjoy the presence of God. There is no better place to be.

You cannot experience the consciousness of the manifestation of God's presence and remain the same.

Importance of God's Presence:

Spending time in God's Presence is very important. Jesus, our perfect example, often withdrew to a lonely place to be alone with God (see Luke 5:16, Matthew 14:23, Luke 6:12). In particular, Music Ministers who lead the people of God in praise and worship need to spend quality time in the presence of God. They need to be in His presence singing praises to Him and worshipping Him, fellowshipping with Him and praying to Him and meditating on His word before leading others in praise and worship or ministering to others in Music. If we fail to do this, we will struggle to lead the people of God to the throne of God – the place where they are aware of and regain the consciousness of the presence of God. Remember, you cannot take people to where you have not been yourself. So spend quality time in God's presence, so that you can minister with more anointing and out of the overflow of the anointing received in God's presence and the river of living water that flows from within you.

John 7:38 "... out of his belly shall flow rivers of living water".

Singing the Right Songs During Praise and Worship Leads to Getting the Right Result

Psalm 123:2 tells us *"Behold, as the eyes of servants look unto the hand of their masters, and as the eyes of a maiden unto the hand of her mistress; so our eyes wait upon the LORD our God,"*

Ministers, especially Music Ministers should spend quality time in the consciousness of the presence of God, waiting on God as His servants, so as to receive from Him what to sing or say during praise and worship. Just like the eyes of a servant look unto his master to receive instructions on what to serve him. Like my little daughter said, you can perceive praise as the food we serve God and worship as the drink we serve Him. This will help to ensure you serve God what He really wants you to serve Him at a given time. Select songs under God. Do not select songs just because you like the songs. When you select songs under the leadership of the Holy Spirit, you will have the right theme or menu that God wants served Him at a set time. After such a great praise and worship section, deliverance, healing, refreshment and other supernatural evidence of the manifestation of the presence of God and His power will be experienced.

True and Anointed Worship

John 4:23 "But the hour comes, and now is, when the true worshipers shall worship the Father in spirit and in truth: for the Father seeks such to worship him."

True and anointed worship is done in Spirit and in Truth. The Spirit talks about The Holy Spirit, and the Truth is Jesus Christ. Worshipping God in God and in God. Spirit to Spirit contact; your human spirit and the Spirit of God that lives inside of you. True Worship is all about Jesus Christ. Galatians 2:20 "... it is no longer I that live, but Christ living in me." Christ in you as a worshipper must increase and be exalted and showcased, while you must decrease. It's all about Christ.

Psalm 103:1 says, "Bless the Lord o my soul and all that is within..." And Matthew 22:37 tells us, "Love the Lord your God with all your heart and with all your soul and with all your mind." When the spirit, soul and body of a worshiper is involved in singing praises to God and worshipping Him, this is the point of true communion (Koinonia). The point of wholehearted devotion. The point of being connected with God and leading others to connect to Him in worship, especially when leading others to sing praises and worship. This is the point of overflowing– "...Out of your belly shall flow rivers of living water." John 7:38".

What a True Worshipper Must Be and More

- A broken vessel, moulded and yielded in submission to God.
- A vessel that has intimate relationship with God.
- A vessel that is aware that the Holy Spirit dwells inside of him or her.
- A vessel that fellowships with the Holy Spirit consistently.
- A vessel that is very aware of the presence of God.
- A vessel that listens to God to hear what He is saying
- A vessel that has direct communication with God.

- A vessel that can see in the Spirit (God opening your eyes of understanding to see and understand spiritual things that can only be spiritually discerned).
- A vessel that can bow in the Spirit not just bowing physically.
- A vessel that can be raptured and Lost in God's presence
- A vessel that can recognize, be aware of and experience the flow of God's anointing.

The yoke is broken because of the anointing Isaiah 10:27.

Anointing makes the difference and anointing breaks the yoke. Anointing does not just give Goosebumps; it breaks the yoke. Yoke of bondage, sickness, poverty and so on. Deliverance, healing, refreshment and other supernatural evidence of the manifestation of the presence and power of God will follow. That is great praise and worship. This is the point when spontaneous things may begin to happen, as the Spirit wills. Like tears,

ANOINTING DOES NOT JUST GIVE GOOSEBUMPS; IT BREAKS THE YOKE.

laughter in the Spirit and so on. But remember, the spirit of the prophet is subject to the prophet (1 Corinthians 14:32).

Chapter Five

Audacity to sing at 'Night'

"Oh that men would praise the LORD for his goodness, and for his wonderful works to the children of men!" (Psalm 107:31 KJV)

What is it that gives the audacity to sing even during a "night" situation experience? This will be our focus in this chapter. As you read on, you will find that it is not just down to one thing. Rather a variety of factors come into play to enable this to happen:

1. **Living a Holy Spirit controlled life:** Although the most difficult time to sing is during a "Night" season, the Holy Spirit can give you the audacity to sing when you live a Spirit Controlled life. So even when

circumstances surrounding you is saying "WEEP" the Spirit of God is saying "SING". When you allow your whole being (spirit, soul and body) to be controlled by the Holy Spirit, nothing can stop you. No Problem can stop you. And no circumstance or adversity can hinder you from worshipping God and singing praises to Him. "*But the natural man receives not the things of the Spirit of God: for they are foolishness unto him: neither can he know them, because they are spiritually discerned."* 1 Cor 2:14.

2. **Knowledge of your identity in Christ**:
   - New creation in Christ. 1 Corinthians 5:17 "therefore if anyone be in Christ, he is a new creature; old things are passed away; behold, all things are become new. Knowing who you are in Christ will give you the audacity to sing even at night.
   - The righteousness of God in Christ Jesus: If you are a believer in Christ Jesus, you are the righteousness of God in Christ Jesus. 2 Corinthians 5:21 says, *"For He made Him who knew no sin to be sin for us, that we might become the righteousness of God in Him."* If you have believed with your heart that Jesus Christ

is the son of God and that He rose from death. And you have confessed with your mouth that Jesus is Lord and accepted Him as the Lord and personal saviour of your life, then you have become the righteousness of God in Christ Jesus. Knowing who you are in Christ will give you the audacity to sing even at night, because you know that God can never forsake the righteous. *Psalm 37:25 "I have been young, and now am old; yet have I not seen the righteous forsaken, nor his seed begging bread."*

- Chosen and called to show forth the Praises of God: 1 Peter 2:9-10 *"But you are a chosen generation, a royal priesthood, a holy nation, His own special people, that you may proclaim the praises of Him who called you out of darkness into His marvellous light; who once were not a people but are now the people of God, who had not obtained mercy but now have obtained* mercy." Knowing your identity in Christ will help you to sing praises to God and worship God, even during a night situation. You are chosen and called to proclaim the praises of God.

- God has raised us up and made us sit together in heavenly places in Christ Jesus. Ephesians 2:6
- We are more than conquerors through Christ Jesus, Romans 8:37.
- We are joint–heirs with Christ, Romans 8:17.

3. **Awareness of the fact that God is thinking of us:** *Psalm 8:4 "What are human beings that you think of them; mere mortals that you care for them?"* God is always thinking of us as believers.

   True life Encounter/Testimony:
   I remember when I lost my car and needed one urgently especially, because of our children who were quite young at the time. And I could not afford a car then. God was thinking about it and God impressed it in the mind of a Pastor friend to give me and my family the only car they had. They sent a message to me and said God told them to give me and my family their car and that we should come and take the car, as they wanted to obey God immediately. They bought another car, afterwards. That is the extent God can go for us as believers to show that He

is thinking about us. The awareness of this fact will give you the audacity to continue to sing praises to God, even during a night season experience.

4. **Adequate knowledge of the power of God:** Believers in Christ carry the power of God. Adequate knowledge of that fact will give you the audacity to sing during a night season experience. John 4:4 says that Greater is He that is in us than he that is in the world. Romans 8:11 "But, If the Spirit of him that raised up Jesus from the dead dwell in you, he that raised up Christ from the dead shall also quicken your mortal bodies by his Spirit that dwells in you" the power of God will quicken your mortal body and you will sing praises to God even during a night season experience, knowing that God has the power to do all things and to give you that supernatural result that you need.

5. **Awareness of the call of God upon your life and your Divine assignment:** *Romans 8:28 says "And we know that all things work together for good to those who love God, to those who are the called according to His purpose."* Having the awareness that all things work together for good to those who love God and are called

according to His purpose will keep you singing praises to God during a night season experience.

Awareness of the call of God upon your life will make you to continue to sing even during a night season. When God calls, He equips. When God gives you a vision, He will make the provision for its accomplishment. Knowing these things will keep you singing praises to God even during a night situation in your life. While in jail in Philippi, Paul and Silas were sure of their calling and divine assignment. And they believed that God would surely see them through. So they dared to sing aloud such that the other prisoners heard them. Jeremiah 1:5 “Before I formed you in the womb, I knew you; and before you came forth out of the womb I sanctified you, and I ordained you a prophet unto the nations.”

6. **Awareness of God’s Love:** Having the awareness that God loves us so much will make you dare to sing praises to Him even during a night season experience. *Jeremiah 31:3 “The LORD hath appeared of old unto me, saying, Yea, I have loved thee with an everlasting love: therefore, with*

lovingkindness have I drawn thee". God's love for us is everlasting.

Romans 5:8 "But God commended his love toward us, in that, while we were yet sinners, Christ died for us." God's love for us is unconditional. He first loved us, even while we were still sinners, when we did not deserve to be loved. This awareness will give you the audacity to sing during a "night" season experience.

7. **Knowledge of the fact that God can give us all things**. Romans 8:32 "*He who did not spare his own Son, but gave him up for us all—how will he not also, along with him, graciously give us all things?"* God gave us His Son and so, God can give us all things.

8. **Letting the word of God dwell in you richly and saturate your whole being**. *Colossians 3:16 says "Let the word of Christ dwell in you richly in all wisdom teaching and admonishing one another in psalms and hymns and spiritual songs, singing with grace in your hearts to the Lord"*. The word of God is powerful. And when you read, study and meditate on the Word to the extent that it dwells in you richly and saturates your whole being, you will surely sing praises to

God, no matter the adversity, storm of life or any kind of "night" season you may be going through. Psalm 46:1-11 says that God is our refuge and strength. God is our ever-present help in time of trouble. God is sovereign. Psalm 91: 1-4. We dwell in the secret place of the Most High and God Himself is our stronghold. Psalm 46:3. And speak to yourself the word of God. And spirituals songs and hymns, making melody in our hearts to God always.

9. **Christian Maturity:** Part of Christian maturity is growing in grace and developing the character of Jesus Christ by exhibiting the fruit of the Spirit – including joy – even when the situation around you is not too good. That is Christian Maturity. And it will help to give you the audacity to sing even at night. *Galatians 5:22-23. "But the fruit of the Spirit is love, joy, peace, patience, kindness, goodness, faithfulness, gentleness, self-control; against such things there is no law."* There is also the joy of the Lord which is

PART OF CHRISTIAN MATURITY IS GROWING IN GRACE AND DEVELOPING THE CHARACTER OF JESUS CHRIST BY EXHIBITING THE FRUIT OF THE SPIRIT – INCLUDING JOY inherent in every born-again believer in Christ Jesus. *Romans 14:17 "For the kingdom of God is not meat and drink; but righteousness, and peace, and joy in the Holy Ghost."* It is called, the joy of the Lord. It comes from within. from inside. And external things cannot stop it. *Nehemiah 8:10* tells us that the joy of the Lord is our strength.

10. **Awareness of God's faithfulness**: God is Faithful *"Thy mercy, O LORD, is in the heavens; and thy faithfulness reacheth unto the clouds." Psalm 36:5.*

11. **Awareness of the fact that we have a High priest that is touched by the feelings of our infirmities**. Hebrews 4:15 "For we have not a high priest which cannot be touched with the feeling of our infirmities; but was in all points tempted like as we are, yet without sin".

12. **Awareness of the truth that God answers prayers:** *Psalm 65:1-2 "Praise is awaiting You, O God, in Zion; And to You the vow shall be performed, You who hear prayer."* This awareness that God answers prayers, will give you the audacity to praise God, even in a "night" situation. *Jeremiah 33:3 "Call to Me, and I will answer you, and*

show you great and mighty things, which you do not know.

13. **God keeps His promise:** Romans 4:21 "And being fully persuaded that, what he had promised, he was able also to perform." Knowledge of the fact that God keeps the promises that he made to His people will keep you singing during a night situation. From Numbers 23:19 we see that God keeps his promise. He is not a man that He should lie, God is not the son of man that He should repent or change. When He says something, He will cause it to come to pass.

14. **Faith:** Just have Faith in God and belief that He will do what He says He will do. Abraham staggered not at the promise of God through unbelief; but was strong in faith, giving glory to God; *Romans 4:20*. Scriptures like this help to remind us and to keep us going, giving glory to God and singing praises to Him during the "night" situation.

15. **God can never be too late:** *Romans 4:19 "And being not weak in faith, he considered not his own body now dead, when he was about an hundred years old, neither yet the deadness of Sarah's womb:"* Abraham held on to God's promises. He refused to consider

his physical condition as being very old and the deadness of his wife, Sarah's womb.

16. **Finding Rest in God:** God is our place of rest. *Psalm 62:5. "Find rest o! my soul, in God alone, my hope comes from him".* Make conscious effort to find rest especially when we are beginning to feel overwhelmed. God is ready to give us rest. *Matt 11:28 "Come to me all ye that are weary and heavy laden and I will give you rest".* Encourage yourself in the Lord and you will have the audacity to sing praise to Him even during a night season experience.

17. **Finding the Peace of God:** John 14:27 *"Peace I leave with you, My peace I give to you; not as the world gives do I give to you. Let not your heart be troubled, neither let it be afraid."* Finding the inner peace of God that passes all understanding, will give you the audacity to sing praises to God even in a "night" situation.

18. **Your past testimonies and that of others**. Surround yourself with people who can testify of the goodness of God. Remember the testimonies of what God did for you in time past. Count your blessings and you will have the audacity to worship God and sing

praises to Him even during a night season experience.

19. **Knowledge of the fact that God can never forget you**: Knowing that God can never forget you as a child of God will give you the audacity to sing praises to God during a night season experience.

    Isaiah 49:15 "Can a woman forget her sucking Child, that she should not have compassion on the son of her womb? Yea, they may forget, yet will I not forget you". During the recent night season experience in my life this particular word of God encouraged me and contributed to what kept me going for about five years. I kept hearing this word of God in my spirit. "I have not forgotten you". And it gave me the audacity to continue to sing praises to God.

20. **Constantly reminding yourself of the fact that God is sovereign:** God is sovereign. God rules in the affairs of men. *Daniel 4:17 "For this has been decreed by the messengers; it is commanded by the holy ones, so that everyone may know that the Most High rules over the kingdoms of the world. He gives them to anyone he chooses--even to the lowliest of people."* God created and controls the universe.

21. **Knowledge of the fact that God loves and rewards sacrificial service:** Praising God during a night season, a time of difficulties, a time you should be weeping and you chose to sing praises to God, is a sacrificial service to God. The PSALMIST demonstrated this in the book of Psalms. Example Psalm, why so downcast o! My soul, put your hope in God and bless the Lord oh my soul...Bless the Lord O! My soul etc. Though He was downcast because of what he was going through, he encouraged himself to sing praises to God and bless the Lord. This knowledge will give you the audacity to sing during a night season experience.

22. **Assurance of the fact that God is with you always:** *Isaiah 43:2-4 "When you pass through the waters, I will be with you; and through the rivers, they shall not overflow you. When you walk through the fire you shall not be burned, nor shall the flame scorch you. For I am the Lord your God..."* There is nothing as reassuring as hearing God, telling you, I am with you always no matter what you are going through. That is enough to give you the audacity to continue singing praises to God even in a night season experience. Also we know that God is with us all the way through

and is working out all things for our good. Romans 8:28.

23. **Knowledge of the fact that God is our Strength:** *Habbakkuk 3:19 "The Sovereign Lord is my strength; He makes my feet like the feet of the deer, He enables me to tread on the heights."* Knowing that God is your strength will give you the audacity to sing even during a night season experience. *Philippians 4:13 "I can do all things through Christ who strengthens me."* and *"The Lord is my strength and song" Psalm 118:14*

24. **It will come to Pass or It will end:** *1 Peter 5:10 "And after you have suffered a little while, the God of all grace, who has called you to his eternal glory in Christ, will himself restore, you, strengthen you and establish you."* The right way to see a "Night" season is to see it in line with the scriptures. It is for a little while and it will come to an end. That is the right perception and seeing it that way, will make you continue to sing praises to God during a night season experience.

25. **Our victory is sure and we are more than Conquerors in Christ:** God has already given us victory. It is just for us to receive our God given victory in Christ. We are

more than conquerors through Christ. Romans 8:37 *"Yet in all these things we are more than conquerors through Him who loved us"*.

26. **God will honour you:** For your shame, God will give you double honour.

27. **Knowing that God will remember you:** Knowing that God will remember you for good will give you the audacity to sing praises to God even in a night situation. *Malachi 3:16 "... and a book of remembrance was written before him for them that feared the LORD, and that thought upon his name."*

28. **God cannot forget our labour of Love:** *Hebrews 6:10 "For God is not unrighteous to forget your work and labour of love, which ye have shewed toward his name, in that ye have ministered to the saints, and do minister."* Knowing that God is not unrighteous to forget your labour of love will give you the audacity to sing praises to God during a night situation.

29. **The Resolution to celebrate God in every situation:** Celebrate what you have and where you are presently, as you cannot be everywhere at

CELEBRATE WHAT YOU HAVE AND WHERE YOU ARE PRESENTLY, AS YOU CANNOT BE EVERYWHERE AT THE SAME TIME.

the same time. Find out the good about that situation or circumstance and enjoy it while it lasts. Example; if you are in-between jobs, that offers you more time to do exploits for God, spend more time with family and friends, while waiting to get back to work. See the good side of every situation and maximize it. Celebrate strength, while working on weakness.

Psalm 113: 1-2 "Praise ye the LORD. Praise, O ye servants of the LORD, praise the name of the LORD. Blessed be the name of the LORD from this time forth and for evermore."

Chapter Six

Great songs come out of 'Night' situation experiences

"He put a new song in my mouth, a hymn of praise to our God. Many will see and fear and put their trust in the Lord." (Psalm 40:3)

Night situation is a difficult time to sing. And the situation may even try to discourage and stop you from worshipping God. But that is the best time to sing praises to God, because great songs come out of night situation experiences. Job 35:10 says "...Where is God my Maker, who gives songs in the night". And David said in *Psalm 40:3 "He put a new song in my mouth, a hymn of praise to our God. Many will see and fear and put their trust in the Lord"*

Most anointed and inspiring songs are songs received during night situation experiences by great gospel artists. Night signifies time of difficulties, adversities, "going through", storm of life, abandonment, loneliness, affliction, and so on. Yet night situation experiences will provide opportunities for you to receive songs from God as you draw close to Him.

NIGHT SIGNIFIES TIME OF DIFFICULTIES, ADVERSITIES, "GOING THROUGH", STORM OF LIFE, ABANDONMENT, LONELINESS, AFFLICTION...

Example of a Song that Came Out of a Night Situation Experience:

Raise A Hallelujah.

Recently, I read an article titled, "The Powerful Testimony Behind Bethel Music's New Song 'Raise A Hallelujah'" which was published on the 8th, February 2019, by Kriza Jo L. Tanduyan. The article revealed the powerful story behind Bethel Music's new song "Raise A Hallelujah". The song which was written by Jonathan and

Melissa Helser members of Bethel Music came out of a night situation, as a powerful declaration over the life of their friend's son, Jaxon.

Jaxon's Kidney got infected by E.coli virus and he was going through blood transfusion and dialysis. Jaxon's parents who had earlier reached out to the church community and friends for prayer and support, sent a message one night that their son, Jaxon was in a critical condition and that they did not think Jaxon will make it.

Jonathan Helser said, that something incredible happened as they were praying for Jaxon. Guess what, a new song came out of their mouth suddenly as they were praying for Jaxon and they continued singing. In the words of Jonathan Helser, they sang against the giant Jaxon was facing.

"I raise A Hallelujah in the presence of my enemy"

"I raise a hallelujah, louder than the unbelief" ...

"I raise a Hallelujah, My weapon is a melody"

"I raise a Hallelujah, heaven comes to fight for me"

They received a miracle, Jaxon was miraculously healed and with countless prayers and medical treatments, Jaxon is well again and healthy.

Examples of Songs that Came Out of My Night Experience

- "Ever present Help": Through my night situation experience, God proved to me that He is ever present with me even in the night situation and in everything I go through. He proved to be my refuge; with me even in the night situation and my ever present help every step of the way.

- I love to sing your praise, Lord.
  The night situation in my life brought me closer to God and made me love to sing God's praises more.

- Jesus, Jesus, Jesus...
  My encounter made me realize more the power in the name of Jesus. The name of Jesus is the greatest and most powerful name. That is why I sing Jesus, Jesus, Jesus. That is the sweetest name.

- "Onumu apugi Ikoya." Means, my mouth cannot tell it all. My mouth cannot tell or narrate what the Lord has done for me, though I try. In order words, what God has done for me is so much that I lack the capability to narrate them all.

A Biblical Example of Singing During a Night Situation

2 Chronicles 20:20-23 *"So they rose early in the morning and went out into the Wilderness of Tekoa; and as they went out, Jehoshaphat stood and said, "Hear me, O Judah and you inhabitants of Jerusalem: Believe in the LORD your God, and you shall be established; believe His prophets, and you shall prosper." And when he had consulted with the people, he appointed those who should sing to the LORD, and who should praise the beauty of holiness, as they went out before the army and were saying: "Praise the LORD, For His mercy endures forever." Now when they began to sing and to praise, the LORD set ambushes against the people of Ammon, Moab, and Mount Seir, who had come against Judah; and they were defeated. For the people of Ammon and Moab stood up against the inhabitants of Mount Seir to utterly kill and destroy them. And when they had made an end of the inhabitants of Seir, they helped to destroy one another".*

In the story above we see that the Israelites were faced with battle, a night situation experience. But it did not stop them from singing praises to God, as God commanded. They continued to sing praises to God and God fought their battle and defeated their enemies for them. Despite the fact that they were faced with battle, they sang about the goodness of God. They sang about the mercies of God and continued to sing praises as the Lord commanded. Sometimes you sing praises to God because you believe the word of God that you sing and other times you sing it until you believe it and it begins to work for you. Either way, I encourage you to dare to sing even at night.

The Israelites continued to sing "For the Lord is good and His mercies endure for ever" even when they were facing battle. They continued to sing as the Lord commanded them until they began to see the manifestation of their God given victory and their enemies began to kill themselves. Do not stop singing the song that God gave you at night, because you have not yet seen the physical manifestation of your God-given victory. Keep on singing.

More reasons to sing Praises to God even at "night"

1. **"Sing," is a divine command** which, when you obey, attracts divine blessings. Psalm 96:1 "Sing to the Lord a new song; sing to the Lord, all the earth". Psalm 95:1 "Come, let us sing for joy to the Lord." We sing praises to God and worship God because He is God. Not necessarily for what He did for us or gave to us.

2. **God inhabits praises.** *Psalm 22:3*. The Hebrew word translated as inhabit is "YSb" which also means to enthrone, to sit and remain sitting, to dwell and implies the idea of ownership and control.

3. **God created us to praise Him.** Revelations 4: 11 says that God created all things for His pleasure. I believe all things includes us all. So give God pleasure by singing songs of praise to Him and by worshipping Him.

4. **Praise is a sacrifice to God.** Hebrews 13:15. *"By him therefore let us offer the sacrifice of praise to God continually, that is, the fruit of our lips giving thanks to his name".*

5. **Praise moves the hand of God and provokes miracles.** *Acts 16:16*

6. **Singing is service to God and Singing is Ministering to God:** Singing is service to God. When we sing to God we render service to the Lord. When you are rendering service unto God, you qualify for His supernatural rewards and miracles. I believe that there are lots of seen and unseen battles that God fought and is still fighting for me, because I am in the service of "Singing for God". 2 chronicles 20:20 God fought for His people while they were singing for Him.

7. **Singing praises to God glorifies God:** The Bible says that whosoever offers praises to God, glorifies God. Psalm 50:23. Singing praises to God glorifies God.

8. **Singing praises to God edifies you and even people around you:** *Ephesians 5:19 "speaking to one another in psalms and hymns and spiritual songs, singing and making melody in your heart to the Lord,".*

9. **Singing praises to God brings joy:** Psalm 63:7" For you have been my help and in the shadow of your wings, I will sing for joy".

10. **Singing songs of Praise to God reduces stress and anxiety.**
    Singing praises to God reduces and eliminates stress and anxiety because it is a demonstration of trust in God. Isaiah 26:3 "You will keep him in perfect peace, whose mind is stayed on you, because he trusts in you".
    Philippians 4:6-7 "Be anxious for nothing, but in everything by prayer and supplication, with thanksgiving, let your requests be made known to God; and the peace of God, which surpasses all understanding, will guard your hearts and minds through Christ Jesus.".

11. **Singing praises to God makes God fight our battles:** When we sing praises to God, God fights our battle, both seen and unseen. 2 chronicles 20:20.

Hosea 4:6 "My people perish for lack of knowledge..." Knowledge will make you dare to sing praises to God no matter the situation.

The Psalmist: Lessons from King David

Night signifies a time of abandonment and loneliness, but that feeling of loneliness and abandonment offers the opportunity to be alone with God. Drawing from my personal experience in walking with God, anytime something great is about to happen or anytime God wants to take me to a greater level or assignment, there is need for preparation, which most times is achieved by being more alone with God in prayer, in praise and in worship. Meditating and spending more time in His presence. This helps to draw me closer to God; to establish a closer and stronger relationship with Him; to become more aware of His power; to become better prepared for the next level; and to receive great songs from Him.

> ...FEELING OF LONELINESS AND ABANDONMENT OFFERS THE OPPORTUNITY TO BE ALONE WITH GOD.

Psalm 40:3 "And he hath put a new song in my mouth, even praise unto our God:" Songs that come out of night situation experiences are usually great songs. For example, most of the songs David the Psalmist wrote were written during night situation experiences. He was careful to make sure that after His lamentation and weeping and sometimes complaints, that he ended up singing about the greatness of God, his trust in God and how he believes that God will see him through and his countenance will change and he will become joyful again. Psalm 42:5 "Why, my soul, are you downcast? Why so disturbed within me? Put your hope in God, for I will yet praise him, my Saviour and God."

God wants all of your being to sing praises to Him and worship Him. How can we do that? Here are few tips that can help:

- **Speak to your soul:** God wants all of your being when singing praises to Him and speaking to your soul to sing praises to God, especially when you are downcast or overwhelmed will help to spur you up to do this. *Psalm 103:1, "Bless the Lord o my soul and all that is within me..."*
- **Remind yourself of all the benefits you receive from God.** Psalm 103:2 "Bless the Lord, O my soul and forget not all His benefits"
- **Put your hope in God** *"...Hope in God, for I shall yet praise Him for the Help of His Countenance." Psalm 42:5*

- **Remind yourself about the following from the book of *Psalms*.**
- Remind yourself that God forgives all your iniquities.
- God heals all your diseases.
- God redeems your life from destruction and you are the redeemed of the Lord.
- God crowns you with lovingkindness and tender mercies and abundant mercy.
- God satisfies our mouth with good things.
- Renews our youth like eagle's.
- The Lord executes righteousness and justice for all who are oppressed.
- He has compassion on us more that our earthly father.
- God satisfies the longing soul and fills the hungry soul with goodness.

Importance of musical skill acquisition:

David not only enjoyed his lone times with God, but He used his lone times to develop himself spiritually, acquire musical skills and write songs. David acquired singing and musical skills which he used for God and which made him well known – such that he was able to minister before the King, Saul. God loves it when we make a joyful noise. He also loves the skills we use to minister in songs to Him. Be encouraged, especially if you are called into the music ministry. Find time and intentionally make effort to develop your musical skills, as you grow spiritually to use it for God. *Psalm 33:3 "Sing to him a new song; play skilfully ..."*

GOD LOVES IT WHEN WE MAKE A JOYFUL NOISE. HE ALSO LOVES THE SKILLS WE USE TO MINISTER IN SONGS TO HIM.

1 Samuel 16:18 "Then answered one of the servants, and said, Behold, I have seen a son of Jesse the Bethlehemite, that is cunning in playing, and a mighty valiant man, and a man of war, and prudent in matters, and a comely person, and the LORD is with him".

David's loneliness during the night season experiences in his life, offered him time to be with God, enabling him to establish a closer relationship with God. It also increased his knowledge of God, and enabled him to receive great songs from God. It also gave him the opportunity to be prepared for greatness, as he had confidence in God and His promises. Psalm 42:8 "Yet the Lord will command his lovingkindness in the day time, and in the night his song shall be with me, and my prayer unto the God of my life".

Psalm 7:17 "I will give thanks to the Lord, because of His righteousness and will sing praise of the name of the Lord Most High".

Establish closer and stronger relationship with God: Do not feel rejected, when close friends and relatives desert you at that time when you go through a night situation. People deserting you at that time helps to remove distractions and offers the opportunity and more time to be alone with God. Spending quality time to sing praises and to worship God. You will have more time to fellowship with God leading to establishing

> DO NOT FEEL REJECTED, WHEN CLOSE FRIENDS AND RELATIVES DESERT YOU AT THAT TIME WHEN YOU GO THROUGH A NIGHT SITUATION.

closer and stronger relationship with God, receive word, direction and vision from God, especially on the way out of the difficulties you are going through. You also get to fellowship more with God and that eliminates the feeling of loneliness and abandonment.

Other Examples of Great Songs that came out of David's Night Situations

Psalm 57: 5 From this verse, we see the song. "Be exalted O God above the heavens". David wrote the song when he fled from Saul in the Cave. David being anointed by God and His victory over Goliath made King Saul jealous. And Saul sought to kill David. This led to David running away to save his life and running to the cave. Though it was a difficult situation, a night situation, David still dared to Sing praises to God and such a great song came out of the night situation David was going through.

Other interesting Psalms are:

Psalm 120:1, A Song of degrees. In my distress I cried unto the LORD, and he heard me.

Psalm 121:1, A Song of degrees. I will lift up mine eyes unto the hills, from whence cometh my help.

Psalm 122:1, A Song of degrees of David. I was glad when they said unto me, let us go into the house of the LORD.

Chapter Seven

Kind of songs to sing and How to sing at 'Night'

Sing the Word of God

The word of God is living and powerful and singing the word of God releases the power of God in your life and situation. Hebrew 4:12 *"For the word of God is living and powerful, and sharper than any two-edged sword, piercing even to the division of soul and spirit, and of joints and marrow, and is a discerner of the thoughts and intents of the heart."*

The Bible further encourages us in *Colossians 3:16 to let the word of Christ dwell in us richly, teaching and admonishing one another in all wisdom, singing psalms and hymns and spiritual songs, with thankfulness in our hearts to God*. Singing the word of God is another way of proclaiming and affirming it. What lyrics is best to sing, other than the word of God?

SINGING THE WORD OF GOD IS ANOTHER WAY OF PROCLAIMING AND AFFIRMING IT.

As you sing the word of God, you shape and frame your life with the words of your song. You shape your situations and your future. Thereby determining the quality of your life.

More reasons why you should sing the word of God:

- Singing the word of God makes available the Power of God. *Hebrew 4:12.*
- The word of God is yes and amen.

  2 Corinthians 1:20.
- The word of God is Spirit and gives life. *John 6:63 "... the words that I speak unto you, they are spirit, and they are life."*
- Singing the word of God puts God in remembrance of His Promises.

Isaiah 43:26 "Put me in remembrance: let us plead together: declare thou, that thou mayest be justified."

- Singing the word brings a confession of hope through the lyrics that is sang
- The word of God can never change, but changes all situations and can do all things. From 2 Chronicles 20:1-22 we see that when the Israelites were faced with battle, they were singing, "For the Lord is good and His mercies endures for ever". That is the scripture, the word of God, and it changed their situation to victory. It may not make sense to the common sense, but that is the word of God. So sing the word of God.

Psalm 138:2 "I will worship toward thy holy temple, and praise thy name for thy lovingkindness and for thy truth: for thou hast magnified thy word above all thy name."

Sing about God and His Attributes

Sing about God. Sing about who God is. Sing about His attributes. God is Almighty. Who can stop the Lord, Almighty? God is Great. God is Holy. He is Awesome. He is powerful. He is merciful. Sing about the goodness and mercies of God. *Psalm 89:1"I will sing of the mercies of the LORD for ever: with my mouth will I make known thy faithfulness to all generations."*

God is good. God is merciful. And we need to sing about this no matter the storm we may be going through in life.

Sing in Tongues/Sing in the Spirit:

1 Corinthians 14:15 "... I will sing with my spirit, but I will also sing with my understanding."

Our understanding is limited, but our spirit is not. So we will sing in our understanding and in the Spirit. If you have received the baptism of the Holy Spirit and you have the spirit of God living inside of you, when you sing in the Spirit you achieve the following:

- You are singing mysteries to God.
- You are saying what you need to say.
- You connect in the spirit realm with what God is doing in your life, (Spirit to spirit contact). *Zechariah 4:6 "...It is not by might, nor by power, but by the Spirit says the Lord of Hosts"*

- You arrange things in the Spirit realm. The Holy Spirit helps you by singing the right things to God, using the right lyrics, because the Holy Spirit knows the will and the mind of God. *"For the Spirit searches all things, yes the deep things of God" 1 Corinthians 2:10*
- You take charge by singing in the Spirit
- You change every unpleasant situation around you.
- You change and harmonize your life with your God given purpose and destiny.
- You receive Revelation from God: *"Eyes has not seen, nor ears heard, nor have entered into the heart of man, the things which God has prepared for those who love Him. But God has revealed them to us through His Spirit..." 1 Corinthians 2:9-10*
- You come in-line with the Will of God, because the Holy Spirit helps us to be in-line with the Will of God.

  1 John 5:14-15 "Now this is the confidence that we have in Him, that if we ask anything according to His will,

> *He hears us. And if we know that He hears us, whatever we ask, we know that we have the petitions that we have asked of Him."*

Sing the name of Jesus:

Philippians 2:9-11 "Therefore God also has highly exalted and given Him the name which is above every name, that at the name of Jesus, every knee should bow of those in heaven and of those on earth and of those under the earth and that every tongue should confess that Jesus is Lord, to the glory of the Father." PROVERBS 18:10 "The name of the Lord is a strong tower, the righteous runs into it and are saved".

Singing the name of Jesus especially during a night situation experience is very reassuring and powerful, because there is power in the name of Jesus. Situations bow at the mention of the name of "Jesus"

The name of Jesus is:

1. **Almighty One** – *"...who is and who was and who is to come, the Almighty." Rev. 1:8*

2. **Alpha and Omega** – *"I am the Alpha and the Omega, the First and the Last, the Beginning and the End." Rev. 22:13*
3. **Advocate** – *"My dear children, I write this to you so that you will not sin. But if anybody does sin, we have an advocate with the Father-Jesus Christ, the Righteous One." 1 John 2:1*
4. **Author and Perfecter of Our Faith** *"Fixing our eyes on Jesus, the author and perfecter of our faith, who for the joy set before Him endured the cross, despising the shame, and has sat down at the right hand of the throne of God." Heb. 12:2*
5. **Authority** – *"Jesus said, 'All authority in heaven and on earth has been given to me." Matt. 28:18*
6. **Bread of Life** – *"Then Jesus declared, 'I am the bread of life. Whoever comes to me will never go hungry, and whoever believes in me will never be thirsty.'" John 6:35*
7. **Beloved Son of God** – *"And behold, a voice from heaven said, "This is my beloved Son, with whom I am well pleased." Matt. 3:17*
8. **Bridegroom** – *"And Jesus said to them, "Can the wedding guests mourn as long as the bridegroom is with them? The days will come when the bridegroom is taken away from them, and then they will fast." Matt. 9:15*

9. **Chief Cornerstone** – *"The stone which the builders rejected has become the chief corner stone." Ps. 118:22*
10. **Deliverer** – *"And to wait for his Son from heaven, whom he raised from the dead, Jesus who delivers us from the wrath to come." 1 Thess.1:10*
11. **Faithful and True** – *"I saw heaven standing open and there before me was a white horse, whose rider is called Faithful and True. With justice he judges and wages war." Rev.19:11*
12. **Good Shepherd** - *"I am the good shepherd. The good shepherd lays down his life for the sheep." John 10:11*
13. **Great High Priest** – *"Therefore, since we have a great high priest who has passed through the heavens, Jesus the Son of God, let us hold fast our confession." Heb. 4:14*
14. **Head of the Church** – *"And he put all things under his feet and gave him as head over all things to the church." Eph. 1:22*
15. **Holy Servant** – *"...and grant that Your bond-servants may speak Your word with all confidence, while You extend Your hand to heal, and signs and wonders take place through the name of Your holy servant Jesus." Acts 4:29-30*

16. **I Am** – *"Jesus said to them, "Truly, truly, I say to you, before Abraham was, I am." John 8:58*
17. **Immanuel** – *"...She will give birth to a son and will call him Immanuel, which means 'God with us.'" Is. 7:14*
18. **Indescribable Gift** – *"Thanks be to God for His indescribable gift."* 2 Cor. 9:15
19. **Judge** – *"...he is the one whom God appointed as judge of the living and the dead." Acts 10:42*
20. **King of kings** – *"These will wage war against the Lamb, and the Lamb will overcome them, because He is Lord of lords and King of kings, and those who are with Him are the called and chosen and faithful." Rev. 17:14*
21. **Lamb of God** – *"The next day John saw Jesus coming toward him and said, "Look, the Lamb of God, who* takes away the sin of the world!" John 1:29
22. **Light of the World** – *"I am the light of the world. Whoever follows me will never walk in darkness, but will have the light of life." John 8:12*
23. **Lion of the Tribe of Judah** – *"Weep no more; behold, the Lion of the tribe of Judah, the Root of David, has conquered, so that he can open the scroll and its seven seals." Rev. 5:5*

24. **Lord of All** – *"For this reason also, God highly exalted Him, and bestowed on Him the name which is above every name, so that at the name of Jesus every knee will bow, of those who are in heaven and on earth and under the earth, and that every tongue will confess that Jesus Christ is Lord, to the glory of God the Father." Phil. 2:9-11*
25. **Mediator** – *"For there is one God, and one mediator between God and men, the man Christ Jesus." 1 Tim. 2:5*
26. **Messiah** – *"We have found the Messiah" (that is, the Christ)." John 1:41*
27. **Mighty One** – *"Then you will know that I, the Lord, am your Savior, your Redeemer, the Mighty One of Jacob." Is. 60:16*
28. **One Who Sets Free** – *"So if the Son sets you free, you will be free indeed." John* 8:36
29. **Our Hope** – *"...Christ Jesus our hope." 1 Tim. 1:1*
30. **Peace** – *"For he himself is our peace, who has made the two groups one and has destroyed the barrier, the dividing wall of hostility," Eph. 2:14*
31. **Prophet** – *"And Jesus said to them, "A prophet is not without honor, except in his hometown and among his relatives and in his own household." Mark 6:4*

32. **Redeemer** – *"And as for me, I know that my Redeemer lives, and at the last He will take His stand on the earth." Job 19:25*
33. **Risen Lord** – *"...that Christ died for our sins according to the Scriptures, that he was buried, that he was raised on the third day according to the Scriptures." 1 Cor. 15:3-4*
34. **Rock** – *"For they drank from the spiritual Rock that followed them, and the Rock was Christ." 1 Cor. 10:4*
35. **Sacrifice for Our Sins** – *"This is love: not that we loved God, but that he loved us and sent his Son as an atoning sacrifice for our sins." 1 John 4:10*
36. **Saviour** – *"For unto you is born this day in the city of David a Saviour, who is Christ the Lord." Luke 2:11*
37. **Son of Man** – *"For the Son of Man came to seek and to save the lost." Luke 19:10*
38. **Son of the Most High** – *"He will be great and will be called the Son of the Most High. The Lord God will give him the throne of his father David." Luke 1:32*
39. **Supreme Creator Over All** – *"By Him all things were created, both in the heavens and on earth, visible and invisible, whether thrones or dominions or rulers or authorities-- all things have been created through Him and for*

Him. He is before all things, and in Him all things hold together..." 1 Cor. 1:16-17

40. **Resurrection and the Life** – *"Jesus said to her, "I am the resurrection and the life. The one who believes in me will live, even though they die." John 11:25*
41. **The Door** – *"I am the door. If anyone enters by me, he will be saved and will go in and out and find pasture." John 10:9*
42. **The Way** – *"Jesus answered, "I am the way and the truth and the life. No one comes to the Father except through me." John 14:6*
43. **The Word** – *"In the beginning was the Word, and the Word was with God, and the Word was God." John 1:1*
44. **True Vine** - *"I am the true vine, and My Father is the vinedresser." John 15:1*
45. **Truth** – *"And you will know the truth, and the truth will set you free." John 8:32*
46. **Victorious One** – *"To the one who is victorious, I will give the right to sit with me on my throne, just as I was victorious and sat down with my Father on his throne." Rev. 3:21*
47. **Wonderful Counsellor**
48. **Mighty God**
49. **Everlasting Father**
50. **Prince of Peace**

"For to us a child is born, to us a son is given, and the government will be on his shoulders. And he will be called Wonderful Counselor, Mighty God, Everlasting Father, Prince of Peace". Isaiah 9:6.

Sing about the Blood of Jesus: The Blood of Jesus speaks better things. Revelation 12:11 "And they overcame him; by the blood of the Lamb and by the word of their testimony..."

Sing about the Holy Spirit: The Holy Spirit is our comforter. He is our Teacher. He leads us into all truth. Sing about Him.

Sing with a pure heart and a heart of gratitude: Singing songs of praise to God and worshipping God starts from the heart. We need to sing with a pure heart. We also need to sing with a heart of gratitude to God – a thankful heart.

> SINGING SONGS OF PRAISE TO GOD AND WORSHIPPING GOD STARTS FROM THE HEART. WE NEED TO SING WITH A PURE HEART.

"But the LORD said to Samuel, "Do not look at his appearance or at his physical stature, because I have refused him. For the LORD does not see as man sees; for man looks at the

outward appearance, but the LORD looks at the heart.". 1 Samuel 16:7.

DESPITE THE DIFFICULT CHALLENGES YOU MAY BE FACING, THERE ARE STILL THINGS TO BE GRATEFUL TO GOD ABOUT.

Despite the difficult challenges you may be facing, there are still things to be grateful to God about. So encourage yourself in the Lord using the word of God. Look at reasons that will help you to develop an attitude of gratitude to sing praises to God. For example, you are alive and have breath in you. The Bible says the living should praise the Lord. Isaiah 38:18-19. Psalm 150:6 "Let everything that has breath praise the LORD. Praise the LORD".

Psalm 113:3

"From the rising of the sun unto the going down of the same the LORD'S name is to be praised."

Chapter Eight

Benefits of singing at 'Night'

"But the God of all grace, who hath called us unto his eternal glory by Christ Jesus, after that ye have suffered a while, make you perfect, stablish, strengthen, settle you."
(1 Peter 5:10)

Singing praises to God and worshiping God during a night situation is a proactive way of celebrating our God given victory in advance, because it precedes miracles, every super-natural result and benefits.

Mountains Melt Like Wax: When we Minister to God by singing praises to Him, especially during a night situation experience, the awareness of His presence in us increases. And as you experience the manifestation of the presence of God, you will begin to see the greatness of God instead of your problem. Your problem which was like a mountain will begin to decrease and melt away. Remember, in the presence of God, mountains melt like wax, Psalm 97:5**.** I have personally experienced this severally. Sometimes it comes like a vision or picture of hope, which reassures us that the problem is gone or that the "mountain" has been removed.

Remember, the spiritual controls the physical. So if you can see it in the spirit realm, then you can be rest assured that the manifestation will come afterwards.

Experience Supernatural Intervention of God and Living in the Miraculous: One of the benefits of singing praises to God during a night season situation is that you will receive supernatural intervention of God. Choose to praise your way through the storms of life and whatever you *go through* and you will definitely achieve supernatural and uncommon results. You will also experience living in the miraculous.

Refocus on God: Psalm 121:1 "I will lift up my eyes to the Hills, from whence cometh my help, my help comes from the Lord..."

Singing praises to God especially during a night season experience, will help us to refocus on God. And what you focus on, you will follow. Learn to look above adversities and focus on God. Worshipping God and singing praises to Him will help you to do this.

Put our trust in God: Psalm 20: 7 "Some trust in chariots... but we will remember the name of the Lord our God" Singing during the "night" season helps us to put our trust in God, not on ourselves nor on our efforts. And not on other persons or Princes, Psalm 146:6. Jeremiah 17:5 says that the arm of flesh will fail you.

Nahum: 1:7 *"The Lord is good, a refuge in times of trouble. He cares for those who trust in Him".*

Lean not on your own understanding: Singing during the "Night" season helps us not to lean on our own understanding, but on God. Proverbs 3:5

Elevation: One of the benefits of singing at night is that it elevates you. Instead of being in a position of where you are in doubt, hopeless, depressed or overwhelmed, you will be elevated to a place of expectation. Ephesians 2:4-6 "But God who is rich in mercy, because of His great love with which He has loved us, even when we were dead in trespasses, made us alive together with Christ and raised us up together and made us sit together in heavenly places in Christ Jesus."

Change in circumstance: Paul and Silas had their circumstance changed when they sang at night. By singing at night, you magnify God instead of the problem. And when God is magnified, he will move on your behalf.

Joy comes in the morning: Psalm 30:5 "Weeping may endure for a night, but joy cometh in the morning". Though we weep at night, it is important to snap out of it as soon as possible and as quickly as we can. Refocus on the promise of God that joy is sure to come in the morning. Take the challenge to sing praise and worship God during your night season and your joy will come speedily.

Faith will Rise: Singing during a "night" season is an act of faith in God. And it pleases God, Hebrew 11:6. It will also cause your faith to rise. Sometimes we are singing something because we believe it and other times we sing it until we begin to believe what we sing, especially when we are singing scriptures or something in line with the scriptures. Note; the kind of song you sing is important. Sing the scriptures, it increases faith.

> SOMETIMES WE ARE SINGING SOMETHING BECAUSE WE BELIEVE IT AND OTHER TIMES WE SING IT UNTIL WE BEGIN TO BELIEVE WHAT WE SING...

Regain your confidence in yourself and in God: The Bible demonstrates this in the book of Psalms. Psalm 43:5 "Why, my soul are you downcast? Why so disturbed within me? Put your Hope in God, for I will yet praise Him, my saviour and my God." This verse shows how singing during the "night" season can help you to regain your self-confidence and your confidence in God.

Celebrating your victory in advance: Singing during the "night" season is a proactive way of celebrating your victory before the physical manifestation. Thanksgiving precedes miracles or manifestation of answered prayer. Dare to sing while waiting on God, instead of weeping.

Strengthened: You are strengthened, when you sing praises to God during a night season instead of weeping. Nehemiah 8:10 "...for the joy of the LORD is your strength."

Psalm 118:14 "The Lord is my strength and my song; He has become my salvation.

Habakkuk 3:19 "*The LORD God is my strength, and he will make my feet like hinds' feet, and he will make me to walk upon mine high places. To the chief singer on my stringed instruments*".

Becoming a Worshipper: Singing praise and worshiping God during a night season can make you become a worshipper. God desires those who will worship Him at all times. *Psalm 34:1 "I will bless the Lord at all times: His praise shall continually be in my mouth"*

Sometimes singing during a night season, turns you into a worshiper and you worship God at all times. Other times, you sing during a night season, because you are a worshiper. You have resolved that you will sing praise and worship God, come what may and at all times. That is a high level.

SOMETIMES SINGING DURING A NIGHT SEASON, TURNS YOU INTO A WORSHIPER AND YOU WORSHIP GOD AT ALL TIMES. OTHER TIMES, YOU SING DURING A NIGHT SEASON, BECAUSE YOU ARE A WORSHIPER

Reduces stress and eliminates anxiety: From Psalm 7, 27, 31, 34, 52 we see that David sang severally to the Lord whenever he was overwhelmed. And this gave him peace and helped him to overcome anxiety.

Philippians 4:6-7 *"Do not be anxious about anything, but in everything by prayer and supplication with thanksgiving let your requests be made known to God and the peace of God, which surpasses all understanding, will guard your hearts and minds through Christ Jesus."*

Peace is what we receive from God when we obey Him and His word by praying and giving thanks instead of being anxious. And as you look up to God by singing praises to Him during the night situation of your life, instead of being anxious, you will not be overwhelmed anymore. Because you are casting your cares and worries on to God. 1 Peter 5:7. And the peace of God that passes all understanding will keep your heart and mind in Christ Jesus. Phil. 4:7.

Divine instruction and direction: 2 Kings 3:15-16, *"But now bring me a musician, and when the musician played, the hand of the Lord came upon him. And he said, "Thus says the Lord..."*

The easiest time to hear from God is when you are singing praises to Him. Worshipping and singing praises during a night situation helps you to receive divine instruction and direction from God easily – which is really needful at such a time.

THE EASIEST TIME TO HEAR FROM GOD IS WHEN YOU ARE SINGING PRAISES TO HIM.

Draw souls to God: When you lift up the name of God by singing praises, God will draw men to himself. Souls will be won for God. *John 12:32 "And I, if I am lifted up from the earth, will draw all peoples to Myself."*

From Acts 16 we see that Paul and Silas won the jailor for Christ after they sang during a night situation in prison.

Produces Endurance/Perseverance:
James 1:2-4 says that the testing of your faith produces endurance. When you take up the challenge to sing during a night situation in your life, knowing that it is the testing of your faith, it will produce endurance. You will develop in your character and maturity as a Christian. That is one of the factors that distinguishes between babes in Christ and matured Christians.

Scientific Proof of the Benefits of Singing

Apart from the spiritual and miraculous benefits of singing, especially during adversity, the benefits of singing have also been proven scientifically as below:

Singing boosts, the immune system

Research has proved that singing helps to boost the immune system. The study, tested professional choir members' blood before and after an hour period of rehearsal, the researchers found out in most cases the amount of proteins in the immune system which function as antibodies, known as Immunoglobulin A. were obviously higher just after singing, which was not so after the members of the choir just listened to music.

Singing can be an excellent form of exercise

Singing can be an excellent form of exercise, because during singing, the human lungs and vocal cords get a workout during the process of singing especially when the right techniques are applied.

Singing helps to develop stronger Diaphragm and stimulates overall circulation

Singing helps to develop stronger Diaphragm and stimulates overall circulation. A greater amount of Oxygen is pulled and used during singing than even while engaging in other forms of exercises. This increases Aerobic Capacity and stamina. Singing also advances Mental Alertness because the improvement of blood circulation and oxygenated blood stream lets oxygen extend to the brain. This can also help people with dementia maintain their memories.

Singing releases positive emotion

During singing, something called Neurochemical is released, which leads to positive emotion. Singing can make you feel happy, regardless of your skill level. Because singing makes you have the feeling of being elated and gain the experience of a greater sense of wellbeing.

Singing is an Anti-depressant

According to research, Singing is a natural anti-depressant. During singing, a chemical called ENDORPHINS is released, that makes you feel good, uplifted and happy. Scientist have also identified that there is a tiny organ in the ear called Sacculus. This organ response to frequencies formed during singing, which creates instantaneous sense of pleasure.

Singing can easily take your mind off problems, troubles and adversities, things that can otherwise make you depressed, thereby improving your frame of mind.

Singing reduces Stress

During singing, the level of stress hormone called Cortisol in the blood stream is reduced, because singing is calming, soothing and releases stored muscles tension.

Singing can help you recover your posture

Singing can help you recover your posture and increase your confidence, with regular practice, rehearsal and performances and progress your social life.

Singing can help you sleep well, hence lullaby. Singing to babies also helps to prepare their brains for language. Singing is also a way of communication and it also increases communication.

Develop the Right Attitude of Singing Praises as a Service to God

Singing praises is a service to God, especially during the night season. It is sacrificial service to the Lord. A sacrifice of praise, the fruit of our lips. It requires a personal, conscious resolution to do it. And it needs to be done with a servant heart, the right attitude and a good motive before God. *Hebrews 13:15. "By him therefore let us offer the sacrifice of praise to God continually, that is, the fruit of our lips giving thanks to his name".*

I believe one of the reasons God called David a man after His heart, is that David had a humble heart and the attitude of singing praises as service to God. *Luke 17:10, "So you also, when you have done everything you were told to do, should say, 'We are unworthy servants; we have only done our duty.'"*

Worshipping God and singing praises to Him in a time of adversity requires a daring attitude. When you do this, you will also experience the following benefits:

1. You will establish a close and stronger relationship with God
2. You will experience God in a different dimension.
3. Your knowledge of God will increase.
4. You will understand God better.
5. God will reveal Himself to you in a greater and different way.
6. Your will experience the power of God in great measure.
7. You will get more awareness of the greatness and glory of God

Conclusion

Revelation of singing Praises and worshipping God in Heaven

Revelation 7: 9 -10 “After this I looked, and there before me was a great multitude that no one could count, from every nation, tribe, people and language, standing before the throne and before the Lamb. They were wearing white robes and were holding palm branches in their hands. And they cried out in a loud voice: “Salvation belongs to our God, who sits on the throne, and to the lamb”.

The book of Revelation reveals to us and gives us the picture of the worship and singing of songs of praise that goes on in heaven. Singing praises to God and worshiping Him is done continuously. There is no time for practice and rehearsals in heaven. So start practicing and rehearsing here on the earth, even during a night season in your life.

SINGING PRAISES TO GOD AND WORSHIPING HIM IS DONE CONTINUOUSLY. THERE IS NO TIME FOR PRACTICE AND REHEARSALS IN HEAVEN.

1 Peter 2:9 says "But you *are* a chosen generation, a royal priesthood, a holy nation, His own special people, that you may proclaim the praises of Him who called you out of darkness into His marvellous light;" We are called by God to proclaim His praises, among other things. So do not put your ladder against the wrong wall by weeping all through a night season experience. Instead, take a step of faith and **sing! Dare to sing even at night.**

The End

REVIEW

The book **"Sing! Dare to Sing @ Night**" is a compendium of supernatural inspirational teachings of a woman whose habitation is not in any other place than in the Holy of Holies. As I read this book, it was difficult to keep it down because of the magnificent spiritual insight I drew from it. Just as the men of God were inspired to write the scriptures, I believe Bisi Udom received inspiration to unfold the mysteries **"Dare to Sing @ Night**." Bisi was a dear student of Living Word Training Centre Aba, Nigeria where the Supernatural is taught.

I found out that the inspiration of the Almighty is palpable on the pages of this book.

I learnt that God wrote the first commandment by Himself, but when Moses broke it, in producing another one, God dictated and Moses wrote. God continues to dictate inside information to His Holy men and women in such a way men cannot stop practicing His presence.

If anyone is in dear need of deliverance, healings, salvation and all manner of divine connection, this is the book to read!!!

BROTHER EMMA OKORIE
President Living Word Ministries/
Chancellor Rhema university
Aba, Nigeria

REFERENCES

Kriza Jo L. Tanduyan, (2019) The Powerful Testimony Behind Bethel Music's New Song 'Raise A hallelujah' Sourced from https://godtv.com/the-powerful-testimony-behind-bethel-musics-new-song-raise-a-hallelujah/. Accessed 12 October 2019.

Scientific benefits of Singing_sourced from https://takelessons.com/live/singing/health-benefits-of-singing. Accessed 29 September 2019.

Fanny Crosby writer of the Hyme "Blessed Assurance" story_sourced from https://www.sermonwriter.com/hymn-stories/blessed-assurance-jesus-mine/ Accessed 12 October, 2019.

Oyakhilome, C. (2016) The Power of your mind, LoveWorld Publishing.

50 Names and Titles of Jesus: Who the Bible Says Christ Is. Sourced from: https://www.crosswalk.com/blogs/debbie-mcdaniel/50-names-of-jesus-who-the-bible-says-christ-is.html accessed October, 2019.

Nweke, L. 2011, Transformed by A Word, AuthorHouse.

Printed in Poland
by Amazon Fulfillment
Poland Sp. z o.o., Wrocław